| Project 7-11 |

Back to Basics

MATHS

for 7-8 year olds

George Rodda

Addition tables

Check the additions in this table.

+	2	4
1	3	5
2	4	6

$1 + 2 = 3$

$1 + 4 = 5$

$2 + 2 = 4$

$2 + 4 = 6$

Fill in these addition tables.

+	3	6	9	12	15
3					
6				15	
9					
12				24	

+	3	5	7
3			
5			
7			
9			

+	7	9	11
7			
9			
11			
13			

+	8	11	14
8			
11			
14			

+	10	13	16
10			
13			
16			

+	11	14	17
11			
14			
17			

+	0	4	8	12	16
0					
4					
8					
12					

+	0	1	2	3	4	5
10						
11						
12						
13						

Length

Ian's handspan is quite small.

It is 10 cm long.

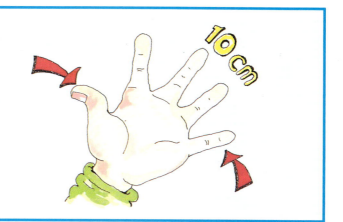

 Fill in the missing numbers for Ian's handspan.

Number of spans	1	2		6		5	3	7
Length	10 cm	cm	40 cm	cm	50 cm		cm	cm

Use Ian's span of 10 cm.

This box is _____ spans long

and _____ spans wide.

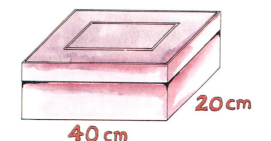

 Write in the lengths in cm.

A frog is ½ span long. _____ cm

A newt is 1½ spans long. _____ cm

A snake is 2½ spans long. _____ cm

A frog and a snake together
would be _____ spans long.

A snake and a newt together
would be _____ spans long.

A snake is _____ spans or _____ cm longer than a frog.

Words for numbers

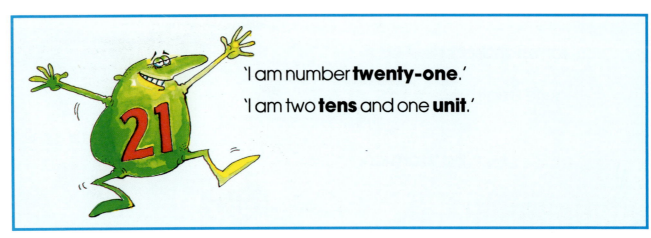

'I am number **twenty-one**.'

'I am two **tens** and one **unit**.'

Write these in figures.

1 thirty-two   **2** sixty-six   **3** thirteen   **4** forty-four

5 one hundred and one _____   **6** ninety-nine _____

Write these numbers in words.

7 41 _____   **8** 33 _____

9 19 _____   **10** 43 _____

11 99 _____   **12** 70 _____

Write in words the value of the number in blue.

13 1**2**0 _____   **14** **3**74 _____

15 44**6** _____   **16** **6**27 _____

17 **1**02 _____   **18** **9**62 _____

Write in words the value of the number in red.

19 7**8**9 _____   **20** **7**89 _____

21 7**8**9 _____   **22** 8**7**9 _____

Taking away

A bus has 19 people on it   19
7 people get off   −7
12 are left on the bus   12

 Finish these sums.

9 − 5 = ☐   12 − 5 = ☐   15 − 5 = ☐
10 − 5 = ☐ 13 − 5 = ☐   16 − 5 = ☐
11 − 5 = ☐ 14 − 5 = ☐   17 − 5 = ☐
10 − 8 = ☐ 13 − 8 = ☐   16 − 8 = ☐
11 − 8 = ☐ 14 − 8 = ☐   17 − 8 = ☐
12 − 8 = ☐ 15 − 8 = ☐   18 − 8 = ☐

```
  19      28      23      13      28      33
 − 7     −20     −19      −4     −18     −12
 ___     ___     ___     ___     ___     ___


  20      17      28      22      20      28
 −11      −9     −19     −12      −4     −17
 ___     ___     ___     ___     ___     ___
```

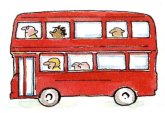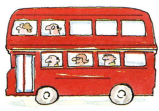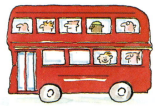

Shapes

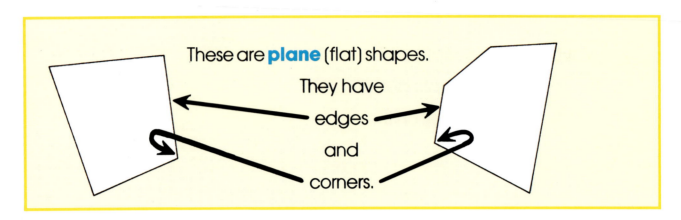

These are **plane** (flat) shapes. They have edges and corners.

✏️ Draw lines to join each shape to its name.

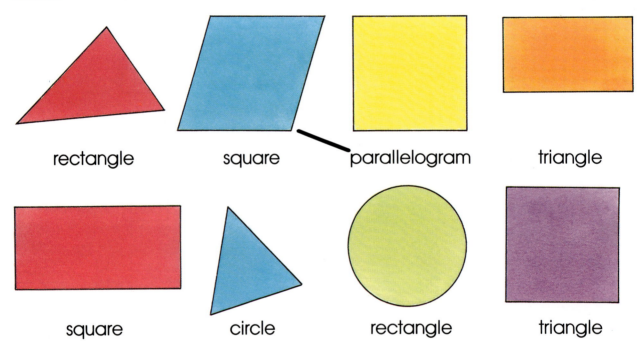

rectangle   square   parallelogram   triangle

square   circle   rectangle   triangle

✏️ Write in the numbers and name for each shape.

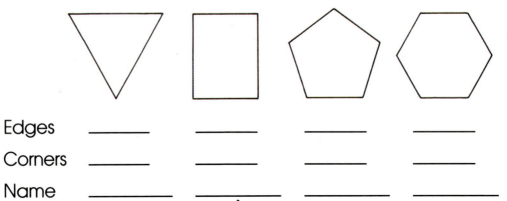

Edges _____   _____   _____   _____
Corners _____ _____   _____   _____
Name   _____   _____   _____   _____

Addition patterns

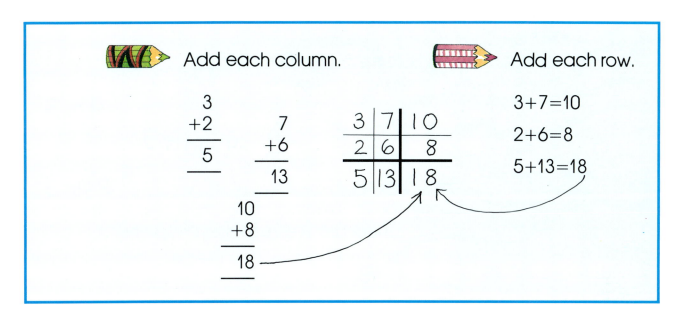

 Fill in these addition squares.

6	5	
5	4	
	20	

8	10	
2	2	

9	11	
4	3	

3	1	1	
3	5	1	
4	2	2	

5	2	3	
1	7	2	
2	2	3	

6	5	1	
4	4	4	
3	1	1	

3	2	1	5	
4	1	5	2	
2	5	4	1	
1	2	4	4	

1	2	3	4	
1	2	3	4	
1	2	3	4	
1	2	3	4	

3	3	3	3	
5	5	5	5	
4	4	4	4	
2	2	2	2	

Addition

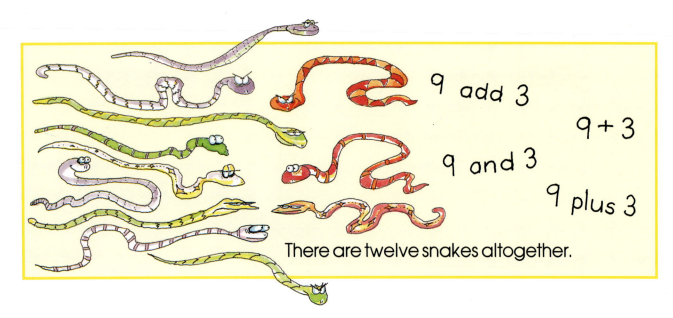

9 add 3
9 + 3
9 and 3
9 plus 3

There are twelve snakes altogether.

 Find the total.

1 27
   +32
   ───

   ───

2 47
   +23
   ───

   ───

3 26
   +34
   ───

   ───

4 126
   +280
   ───

   ───

5 23 + 17
   = ___

6 38 add 51
   = ___

7 62 and 29
   make ___

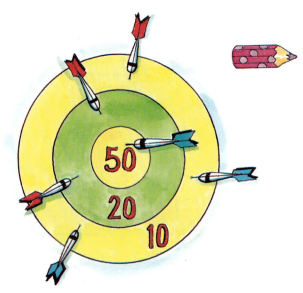

Write in the missing number.

8 The total score for the three red darts is ___

9 The total score for the three blue darts is ___

10 The total score for the six darts is ___

11 Draw 3 black darts to score 80.

12 Draw 3 green darts to score 120.

Ten pence

This 10p coin can be exchanged for one 2p coin and eight 1p coins.

10p → 1 2p and 8 1p

✏️ Write the number in each box.

10p → ☐ 2p and 6 1p   10p → ☐ 2p and 4 1p

10p → ☐ 2p and 2 1p   10p → 4 2p and ☐ 1p

10p → ☐ 5p and 5 1p   10p → ☐ 5p

10p → ☐ 2p and 1 1p and ☐ 5p

✏️ Write the coin value in each circle.

10p → 10 p   10p → 2 p

10p → 3 p and 4 p   10p → 1 p and 5 p

10p → 1 p and 1 p and 3 p

Subtraction

Someone has taken 4 cakes.

9 − 4

subtract 4 from 9

9 minus 4

9 take away 4

There are 5 cakes left.

 Work these out.

| 1 | 28
−17 | 2 | 46
−17 | 3 | 34
−17 | 4 | 123
−24 |

5 32 − 9
 = ____

6 41 take away 20
 = ____

7 39 minus 19
 = ____

8 Subtract 15 from 40

9 427 take away 419

Tom's newspaper round is:

High Road	15 papers
Low Road	38 papers
Main Street	57 papers

 Write in the missing numbers.

10 Tom delivers ____ more papers in Main Street than Low Road.

11 Tom delivers ____ less papers in High Road than Low Road.

12 Tom delivers ____ less papers in High Road than Main Street.

A number line

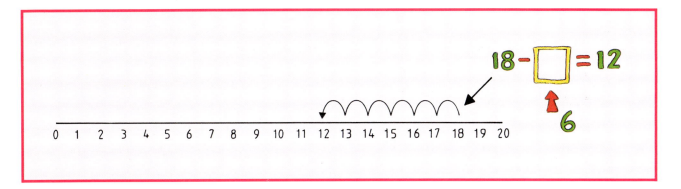

 Use the number line to help you fill in the missing numbers.

1 16 + 2 = ☐   **2** 9 + 9 = ☐   **3** 9 + 8 = ☐

4 16 − 2 = ☐   **5** 9 − 9 = ☐   **6** 9 − 8 = ☐

7 7 + ☐ = 15   **8** 15 − ☐ = 7   **9** 15 − ☐ = 8

10 13 + ☐ = 17   **11** 17 − ☐ = 13   **12** 17 − 13 = ☐

13 18 − 11 = ☐   **14** 11 + 7 = ☐   **15** 18 − 7 = ☐

16 14 − ☐ = 11   **17** 14 + ☐ = 19   **18** 14 − ☐ = 9

19 10
    − 3
    ───

20 18
    − ☐
    ───
     17

21 19
    − ☐
    ───
     18

22 18
    + ☐
    ───
     20

23 11
    + ☐
    ───
     20

24 12
    + ☐
    ───
     20

25 13
    + ☐
    ───
     20

26 14
    + ☐
    ───
     20

27 I have 20p and spend 9p. I have ☐ p left.

28 I started shopping with 20p and now have 16p left. I spent ☐ p.

Multiplication tables

$4 \times 2 = 8$

X	2	3
4	8	12
5	10	15

$4 \times 3 = 12$

$5 \times 2 = 10$

$5 \times 3 = 15$

 Fill in these multiplication tables.

X	2	3	4
2	4		
3			
4			
5			20

X	7	8	9
3			
4			
5			
6			

X	0	2	4	6
0				
2				
4				
6				

X	1	3	5	7
1				
3				
5				
7				

X	6	8	10	12
1				
2				
3				
4				
5				

X	5	7	9
1			
2			
3			
4			
5			

X	1	2	3	4
5				
9				
6				

X	3	2	6	5
3				
5				
7				

X	3	4	5	6
2				
4				
6				

Fractions

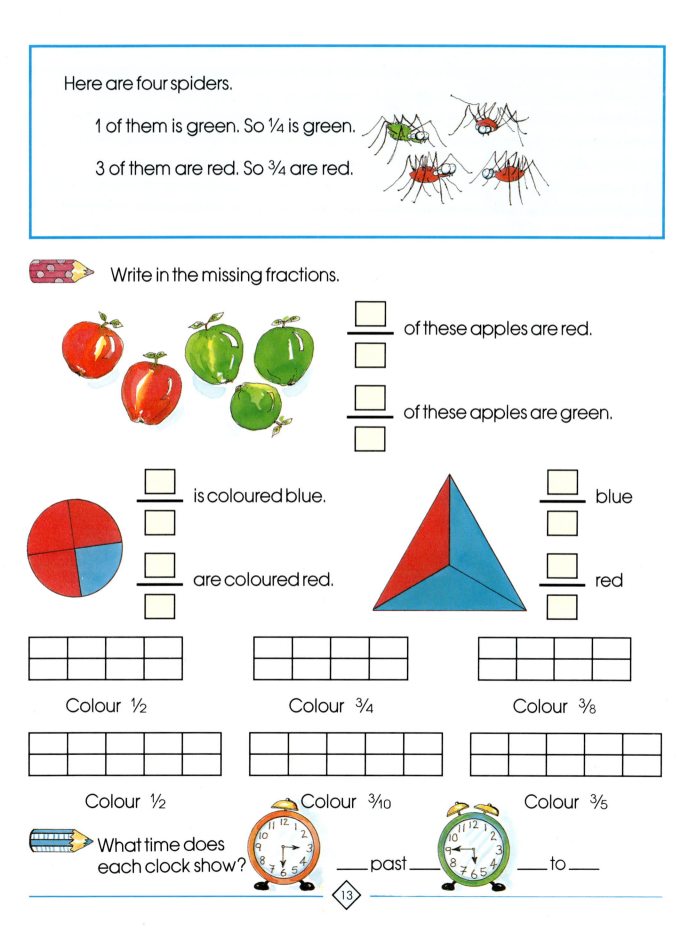

Here are four spiders.

1 of them is green. So ¼ is green.

3 of them are red. So ¾ are red.

Write in the missing fractions.

☐/☐ of these apples are red.

☐/☐ of these apples are green.

☐/☐ is coloured blue.

☐/☐ are coloured red.

☐/☐ blue

☐/☐ red

Colour ½   Colour ¾   Colour ⅜

Colour ½   Colour ³⁄₁₀   Colour ⅗

What time does each clock show? ___ past ___   ___ to ___

Doubling

Double 4 is 2×4
$\qquad = 8$

 Find the total number of spots.

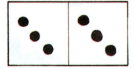
$2 \times 3 = \bigcirc$

$2 \times 4 = \boxed{8}$

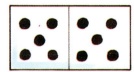
$2 \times 5 = \bigcirc$

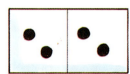
$2 \times 2 = \bigcirc$

$2 \times 0 = \bigcirc$

$2 \times 1 = \bigcirc$

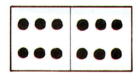
$2 \times 6 = \bigcirc$

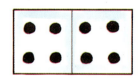
$2 \times 4 = \bigcirc$

The red parts on these boards score **double**.

 Find the total for the three darts on each board.

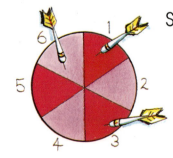

Score: 2×1
$\qquad + 6$
$\qquad + 2 \times 3$

Total ☐

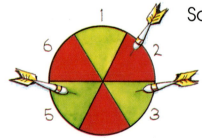

Score:
$\qquad +$
$\qquad +$

Total ☐

 Fill in these doubling patterns.

1, 2, 4, ☐, 16   3, ☐, ☐, 24

5, ☐, 20, ☐   7, ☐, 28, ☐

Using twelve

Pat says that it is time for lunch.

It is five past twelve.

Fill in the missing numbers.

10 + ☐ = 12   2 + ☐ = 12   12 − 10 = ☐

12 − 2 = ☐   12 + ☐ = 22   12 − 8 = ☐

Finish drawing 12 counters to make a **6** by **2** pattern.

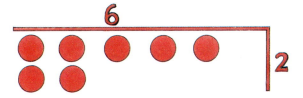

Draw counters for a **2** by **6** pattern.

Draw counters for a **3** by **4** pattern.

Draw counters for a **4** by **3** pattern.

Multiplication

$6 \times 2 = 2 + 2 + 2 + 2 + 2 + 2 = 12$

$4 \times 6 = 6 + 6 + 6 + 6 = 24$

 Fill in the missing numbers and work out the answers.

1 $4 \times 3 = 3 + \bigcirc + \bigcirc + \bigcirc$
= ☐

2 $4 \times 5 = 5 + \bigcirc + \bigcirc + \bigcirc$
= ☐

3 $4 \times 2 = \bigcirc + \bigcirc + \bigcirc + \bigcirc$
= ☐

4 $2 \times 6 = \bigcirc + \bigcirc$
= ☐

5 $3 \times 10 = \bigcirc + \bigcirc + \bigcirc$
= ☐

6 $3 \times 8 = \bigcirc + \bigcirc + \bigcirc$
= ☐

7 $6 \times 5 = \bigcirc + \bigcirc + \bigcirc + \bigcirc + \bigcirc + \bigcirc = $ ☐

8 $5 \times 6 = \bigcirc + \bigcirc + \bigcirc + \bigcirc + \bigcirc = $ ☐

9 $7 \times 4 = \bigcirc + \bigcirc + \bigcirc + \bigcirc + \bigcirc + \bigcirc + \bigcirc = $ ☐

10 $5 \times 3 = $ ☐   **11** $3 \times 5 = $ ☐   **12** $4 \times 4 = $ ☐

13 $2 \times 9 = $ ☐   **14** $9 \times 2 = $ ☐   **15** $2 \times 10 = $ ☐

16 $6 \times 3 = $ ☐   **17** $4 \times 6 = $ ☐   **18** $3 \times 7 = $ ☐

Fractions

Ian's share of the cake is one quarter.

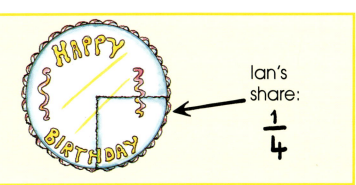

Ian's share: $\frac{1}{4}$

 Use the lines on this cake to help you shade ½ of it red and ⅓ of it blue.

 Use a ruler to measure the length of each piece of string.

 Mark **X** on each piece of string to show:

Length

___ cm ———————————————————— ½ of it

___ cm ———————————————— ½ of it

___ cm ——————————————— ⅓ of it

___ cm —————————————— ¼ of it

This box contains 12 pieces of fudge.

 Fill in the answers.

½ of the box contains ___ pieces

¼ of the box contains ___ pieces

¾ of the box contains ___ pieces

⅓ of the box contains ___ pieces

Time

5 past 12   10 past 12

The difference in time between these clocks is 5 minutes.

 Use the clock faces to help you write down the number of minutes between the two times.

2 o'clock and 10 past 2. ____ minutes

2 o'clock and a quarter past 2. ____ minutes

2 o'clock and 20 past 2. ____ minutes

A quarter past 1 and half past 1. ____ minutes

Half past 1 and a quarter to 2. ____ minutes

1 o'clock and 2 o'clock. ____ minutes

 Draw an arrow round each clock face to show

clockwise    anti-clockwise

My watch is 10 minutes **fast**. It shows 12 o'clock.

The time is _____

My watch is 15 minutes **slow**. It shows ½ past 1.

The time is _____

More or less

4 **is more than** 2

3 **is less than** 7

6 **is equal to** 2 × 3

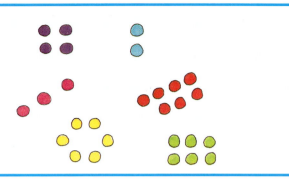

 Put in the correct words from

is more than   **is less than**   **is equal to**

3 × 3 [_____] 2 × 3   2 × 2 [_____] 2 × 2

5 × 3 [_____] 6 × 2   3 + 3 [_____] 3 × 3

10 × 0 [_____] 0 × 6   4 × 5 [_____] 2 × 10

 Write down the total length.

4 spans of 20 cm   4 spans of 21 cm   4 spans of 19 cm

= _____ cm   = _____ cm   = _____ cm

Which answer is more than the other two? _____ cm

Which answer is less than the other two? _____ cm

What is my number?

My number is 3 less than 5 × 3. It is _____

My number is 5 more than 3 × 5. It is _____

My number is 7 more than 6 + 7. It is _____

My number is less than 4 × 2 but more than 2 × 3.

It is _____

Millimetres (mm) and centimetres (cm)

___ This line is 1 cm or 10 mm long.
_____ This line is 2 cm or 20 mm long.
_____ This line is 3 cm or 30 mm long.

Write these lengths in mm.

1 4 cm = ☐ mm   **2** 5 cm = ☐ mm   **3** 6 cm = ☐ mm

4 7 cm = ☐ mm   **5** 8 cm = ☐ mm   **6** 9 cm = ☐ mm

7 ½ cm = ☐ mm   **8** 2½ cm = ☐ mm   **9** ¹⁄₁₀ cm = ☐ mm

Write these mm as cm.

1 30 mm = ☐ cm   **2** 10 mm = ☐ cm   **3** 15 mm = ☐ cm

Add these mm and change the answers to cm.

1 5 mm
  + 15 mm
  ___ mm = ☐ cm

2 25 mm
  + 15 mm
  ___ mm = ☐ cm

3 14 mm
  + 16 mm
  ___ mm = ☐ cm

4 20 mm
   23 mm
  + 37 mm
  ___ mm = ☐ cm

Days and dates

	July				
Mon		7	14	21	28
Tues	1	8	15	22	29
Wed	2	9	16	23	30
Thurs	3	10	17	24	31
Fri	4	11	18	25	
Sat	5	12	19	26	
Sun	6	13	20	27	

This is a calendar page for July

 Answer these questions.

How many days are there in July? _____ days

What is the day

    7 days after Thursday 3rd July? _____ day

    The date will then be _____ July.

What is the day

    5 days after Thursday 3rd July? _____ day

    The date will then be _____ July.

What is the day

    6 days before Friday 18th July? _____ day

    The date will then be _____ July.

On this calendar page shade in red all the **odd** numbers.

On this calendar page shade in blue all the **even** numbers.

	November				
Mon		5	12	19	26
Tues		6	13	20	27
Wed		7	14	21	28
Thurs	1	8	15	22	29
Fri	2	9	16	23	30
Sat	3	10	17	24	
Sun	4	11	18	25	

	February				
Mon		5	12	19	26
Tues		6	13	20	27
Wed		7	14	21	28
Thurs	1	8	15	22	
Fri	2	9	16	23	
Sat	3	10	17	24	
Sun	4	11	18	25	

Sharing

12 ÷ 3 = 4

Ian, Tom and Mary can have 4 sweets each.

Ian's share   Tom's share   Mary's share

 Write down the answers.

1. 8 ÷ 4 = ☐
2. 8 ÷ 2 = ☐
3. 12 ÷ 2 = ☐
4. 12 ÷ 6 = ☐

5. 15 ÷ 3 = ☐
6. 15 ÷ 5 = ☐
7. 16 ÷ 2 = ☐
8. 16 ÷ 4 = ☐

9. 14 ÷ 2 = ☐
10. 14 ÷ 7 = ☐
11. 18 ÷ 9 = ☐
12. 18 ÷ 2 = ☐

13. 35 ÷ 5 = ___
14. 21 ÷ 3 = ___
15. 28 ÷ 4 = ___
16. 28 ÷ 7 = ___

17. Ian and Mary share 18 apples.
    How many do they have each?   ___ apples

18. Tom, Mary and Ian have equal shares of 27 apples.
    How many do they have each?   ___ apples

 Fill in the missing numbers.

19. 8 ÷ ☐ = 2
20. 10 ÷ ☐ = 5

Weight

You can weigh yourself on scales like these.

Mr Jones weighs 120kg, Mrs Jones weighs 65kg, Tammy weighs 35kg and Ian weighs 40kg.

 Find the total weight for:

1	Mrs Jones	65 kg	2	Tammy	kg	3	Mr Jones	kg
	Tammy +	35 kg		Ian +	kg		Mrs Jones +	kg
		kg			kg			kg

4	Mr Jones	kg	5	Mr Jones	kg	6	Mrs Jones	kg
	Ian +	kg		Tammy +	kg		Ian +	kg
		kg			kg			kg

 Find the difference in weight for:

7	Mrs Jones	kg	8	Ian	kg	9	Mr Jones	kg
	Tammy −	kg		Tammy −	kg		Mrs Jones −	kg
		kg			kg			kg

10	Mrs Jones	kg	11	Mr Jones	kg	12	Mr Jones	kg
	Ian −	kg		Ian −	kg		Tammy −	kg
		kg			kg			kg

13 Find the total weight of the family.   120 kg + 65 kg + 35 kg + 40 kg = _____ kg

Twenty pence

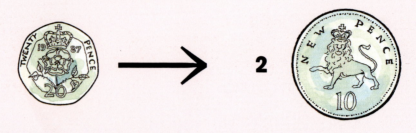

20p can be made up from two 10p coins.

Write the number of coins needed in each box.

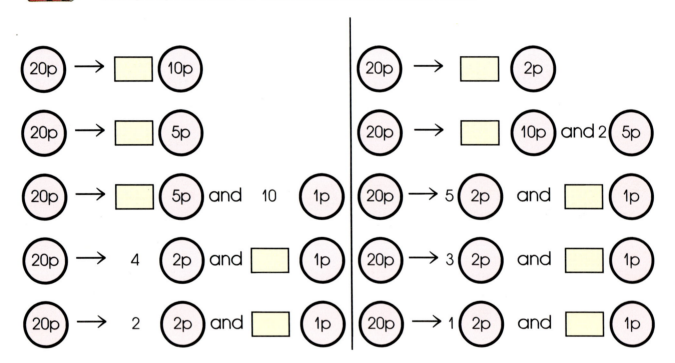

Write the coin value in each circle.

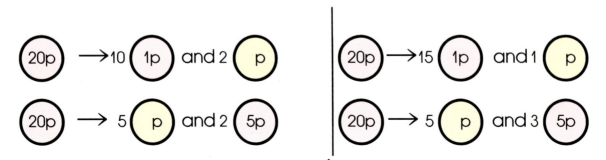

Squares

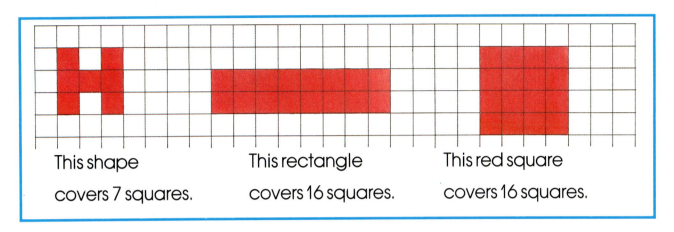

This shape covers 7 squares. This rectangle covers 16 squares. This red square covers 16 squares.

How many squares are covered by these shapes?

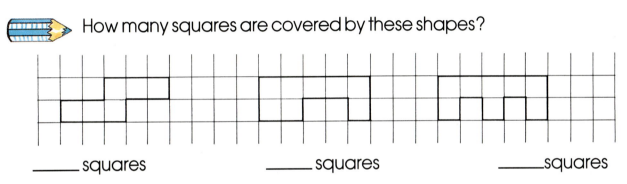

____ squares   ____ squares   ____ squares

On these squares draw the letter:

covering **5** squares   covering **6** squares   covering **7** squares

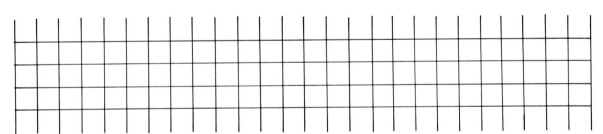

On these squares draw:

a **rectangle** covering **8** small squares   a **rectangle** covering **14** small squares   a **square** covering **9** small squares

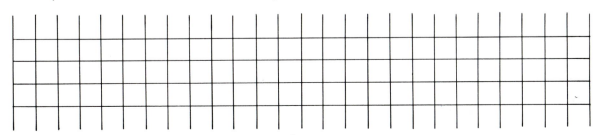

Money

This is a 5p coin.  It is happy to be used with other coins.

 Use **one** coin to finish.

10p = 5p + ☐ p   10p = 8p + ☐ p

10p − 5p = ☐ p   10p = 12p − ☐ p

5p = 15p − ☐ p   20p − 10p = ☐ p

10p − 5p − 3p = ☐ p   10p − 5p − 5p + 2p = ☐ p

10p + 5p − 10p = ☐ p   10p − 5p − 2p − 1p = ☐ p

 How much is there in each purse?

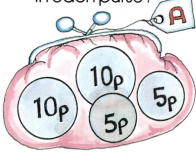
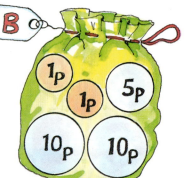
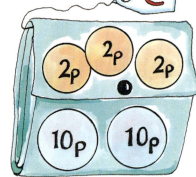

Purse A _____ p   Purse B _____ p   Purse C _____ p

Which purse holds the most money? Purse _____

Which purse holds the least money? Purse _____

Purse B − Purse C is worth _____ p   Purse A − Purse C is worth _____ p

Graphs

This is a graph showing how Ian spends his day.

 Write down the number of hours for Ian.

Bed _____ hours   School _____ hours

Watching TV _____ hours   Travelling _____ hours

Mealtimes _____ hours   Working _____ hours

The total time spent by Ian at school and in bed is _____ hours.

The total time spent by Ian travelling and eating is _____ hours.

 Finish drawing this block graph showing the number of people in each of these families.

Number in family:

Smith	8
Jones	3
Brown	7
Aziz	5
M'Ginty	4
Petra	5

Solids

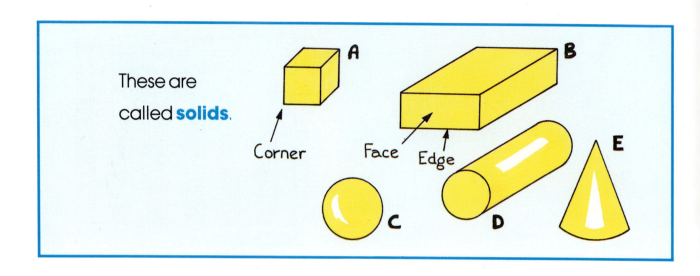

These are called **solids**.

The names of the solids are

sphere, **cylinder**, **cone**, **cuboid** and **cube**.

Put the correct name alongside each letter.

A _____   B _____   C _____

D _____   E _____

For solid A: How many edges has it? _____

How many faces has it? _____

How many corners has it? _____

What is the shape of each face? _____

For solid B: How many edges has it? _____

How many faces has it? _____

How many corners has it? _____

What is the shape of each face? _____

Use this rectangle and the dots to help you draw a cuboid.

Shopping

What is the cost?

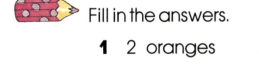 Fill in the answers.

1 2 oranges ____ p **2** 2 lollies ____ p **3** 9 chocos ____ p **4** 3 cones ____ p

5 3 lollies ____ p
   2 chocos ____ p
   Total ____ p

6 3 cones ____ p
   2 oranges ____ p
   Total ____ p

7 4 lollies ____ p
   1 orange ____ p
   Total ____ p

8 2 cones ____ p
   3 lollies ____ p
   1 choco ____ p
   Total ____ p

9 2 oranges ____ p
   1 choco ____ p
   3 cones ____ p
   Total ____ p

10 3 oranges ____ p
   1 cone ____ p
   2 chocos ____ p
   Total ____ p

11 How many chocos can I buy for 50p? ____
12 How many cones can I buy for £1? ____
13 How many oranges can I buy with £1? ____
14 How many chocos can I buy with £1? ____

Fifty pence

This is a 50p coin.

Two of them are worth £1.

 Write in the missing numbers.

From 50p I spend	40p	30p	20p	10p
My change will be	10p	p	p	p

From 50p I spend	45p	35p	25p	15p	5p
My change will be	p	p	p	p	p

 Write the answers.

33p + 17p = ☐ p   23p + 27p = ☐ p   13p + 37p = ☐ p   3p + 47p = ☐ p

50p − 19p = ☐ p   50p − 29p = ☐ p   50p − 39p = ☐ p   50p − 49p = ☐ p

50p − 42p = ☐ p   50p − 32p = ☐ p   50p − 22p = ☐ p   50p − 12p = ☐ p

5p × 10 = ☐ p   10p × 5 = ☐ p   25p + 25p = ☐ p   ½ of £1 = ☐ p

My change from 50p was 41p. How much did I pay? ☐ p

A pen cost 19p. How much change will I need from 50p? ☐ p

Litres

4 cups can be filled from 1 litre.
Each cup holds ¼ litre.

 Write the number of cups.

	1	2	3	4	5	6	7	8	litres
will fill	4								cups.

From 1½ litres I can fill ☐ cups.

From 2½ litres I can fill ☐ cups.

 Write the number of litres.

	4	6	8	10	12	14	16	cups can be
filled from		1½						litres.

What fraction of a litre is 2 cups? ☐

 Write the number of cups which can be filled from:

1	2	3	4	5	6	7	½-litre cartons.
	4					14	cups

 Write in the missing numbers.

	1	2	3	4	2-litre cartons
will fill	8				cups.

Which is the larger, 5 cups or 2 litres? _____

Answers

To Parents:
We have not provided *all* the answers here. We suggest that items to be drawn should be checked by you. In the case of activities where calculations are performed by your child, it would be good practice to get him/her to use a calculator to check the answers.

Page 2
6 9 12 15 18   6 8 10   14 16 18
9 12 18 21   8 10 12   16 18 20
12 15 18 21 24   10 12 14   18 20 22
15 18 21   27   12 14 16   20 22 24

16 19 22   20 23 26   22 25 28
19 22 25   23 26 29   25 28 31
22 25 28   26 29 32   28 31 34

0 4 8 12 16   10 11 12 13 14 15
4 8 12 16 20   11 12 13 14 15 16
8 12 16 20 24   12 13 14 15 16 17
12 16 20 24 28   13 14 15 16 17 18

Page 3
20, 4, 60, 30, 70
4, 2
5, 15, 25, 3, 4, 2, 20

Page 4
32, 66, 13, 44
101, 99

forty-one   thirty-three
nineteen   forty-three
ninety-nine   seventy
twenty   three hundred
six   six hundred
one hundred   nine hundred
nine   eighty
seven hundred   eight hundred

Page 5
4 7 10
5 8 11
6 9 12
2 5 8
3 6 9
4 7 10
12 8 4 9 10 21
9 8 9 10 16 11

Page 6
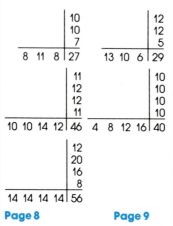

3, 4, 5, 6,
3, 4, 5, 6,
triangle, rectangle, pentagon, hexagon

Page 7
```
   |11        |18
   | 9        | 4
11 | 9     10 12|22

      |12          | 5
      |12          | 9
      | 5          | 8
13 10 6|29    10 8 4|22
```

```
  |10          |12
  |10          |12
  | 7          | 5
8 11 8|27   13 10 6|29

  |11          |10
  |12          |10
  |12          |10
  |11          |10
10 10 14 12|46   4 8 12 16|40

  |12
  |20
  |16
  | 8
14 14 14 14|56
```

Page 8
59, 70, 60, 406
40, 89, 91
50, 70, 120
50, 20, 10
50, 50, 20

Page 9
2 3
4 2
1 2
2 1
1 5
2, 1, 5, 1
2, 5, 1

Page 10
11, 29, 17, 99
23, 21, 20
25, 8
19
23
42

Page 11
18, 18, 17
14, 0, 1
8, 8, 7
4, 4, 4
7, 18, 11
3, 5, 5
7, 1, 1, 2
9, 8, 7, 6
11   4

Page 12
```
   6   8       21 24 27
   6   9 12    28 32 36
   8  12 16    35 40 45
  10  15       42 48 54

  0  0  0  0      1  3  5  7
  0  4  8 12      3  9 15 21
  0  8 16 24      5 15 25 35
  0 12 24 36      7 21 35 49

  6  8 10 12      5  7  9
 12 16 20 24     10 14 18
 18 24 30 36     15 21 27
 24 32 40 48     20 28 36
 30 40 50 60     25 35 45

  5 10 15 20      9  6 18 15
  9 18 27 36     15 10 30 25
  6 12 18 24     21 14 42 35

  6  8 10 12
 12 16 20 24
 18 24 30 36
```

Page 13
2/5
3/5
¼, ¾, ⅔, ⅓
½ past 3, ¼ to six

Page 14
6, 10, 4
0, 2, 12, 8
14   2 × 2 + 3 + 5 = 12
8   6   12
10   40   14   56

Page 15
2, 10, 2
10, 10, 4

Page 16
3, 3, 3   5, 5, 5
12   20
2, 2, 2, 2   6, 6
8   12
10, 10, 10   8, 8, 8
30   24
5, 5, 5, 5, 5, 5, 30
6, 6, 6, 6, 6, 30
4, 4, 4, 4, 4, 4, 4, 28
15, 15, 16
18, 18, 20
18, 24, 21

Page 17
10, 8, 9, 8
6, 3, 9, 4

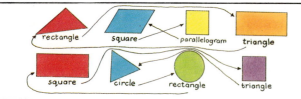

Page 18
10, 15, 20   10 to 12
15, 15, 60   ¼ to 2

Page 19
is more than   is equal to
is more than   is less than
is equal to   is equal to
80, 84, 76
84, 76
12, 20, 20, 7

Page 20
40, 50, 60
70, 80, 90
5, 25, 1
3, 1, 1½
20, 2, 40, 4
30, 3, 80, 8

Page 21
31
Thurs
10th
Tues
8th
Satur
12th

Page 22
2, 4, 6, 2
5, 3, 8, 4
7, 2, 2, 9
7, 7, 7, 4
9
9
4, 2

Page 23
```
         35   120
         40    65
100      75   185
120     120    65
 40      35    40
160     155   105
 65      40   120
 35      35    65
 30       5    55
```

Page 24
2, 10
4, 1
2, 10
12, 14
16, 18
5, 5
2, 1

Page 25
6, 8, 8

Page 26
5, 2
5, 2
10, 10
2, 2
5, 2
30, 27, 26
A
C
1, 4

Page 27
10, 6
3, 2
2, 1
16
4

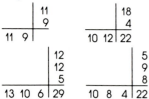

Page 28
A Cube, B Cuboid, C Sphere
D Cylinder, E Cone
12
6
8
Square
12
6
8
Rectangle

Page 29
10, 30, 90, 60
45   60   60
20   10   5
65   70   65
40   10   15
45   10   20
10   60   20
95   80   55
5
5
20
10

Page 30
20, 30, 40
5, 15, 25, 35, 45
50, 50, 50, 50
31, 21, 11, 1
8, 18, 28, 38
50, 50, 50, 50
9
31

Page 31
8, 12, 16, 20, 24, 28, 32
6
10
1, 2, 2½, 3, 3½, 4
½
2, 6, 8, 10, 12
16, 24, 32
2 litres